Earl of Chesterfield,

Worldly Wisdom

Being Extracts from the Letters of the Earl of Chesterfield to His Son

Earl of Chesterfield,

Worldly Wisdom
Being Extracts from the Letters of the Earl of Chesterfield to His Son

ISBN/EAN: 9783337136437

Printed in Europe, USA, Canada, Australia, Japan

Cover: Foto ©ninafisch / pixelio.de

More available books at **www.hansebooks.com**

WORLDLY WISDOM

Being Extracts from the Letters of the Earl
of Chesterfield to His Son

Selected and Illustrated by *W. L. SHEPPARD*

R . H . R·U S S E L L

N E W Y O R K Mdcccxcix

THE WORLDLY WISDOM OF PHILIP DORMER STANHOPE EARL OF CHESTERFIELD

BIOGRAPHICAL NOTE

L ORD CHESTERFIELD was born in September, 1694. His father disliked him and the son was brought up by his grandmother, the Marchioness of Halifax, a good and accomplished woman, who undoubtedly formed his tastes, and helped to form his morals. These, according to the statements of some of his contemporaries, were not as bad as the noble lord made them appear. They were asserted to be creatures of his imagination, given as matters of fact and used as warnings to his son; on whom, as is well known, warnings and precepts were alike thrown away.

With frank egotism, the Earl says of himself: "At the University I was an absolute pedant. When I would be facetious I quoted Martial; when I talked my best I imitated Horace; and when I aimed to be a fine gentleman I quoted Ovid. I was insolent, a great talker, proud and peremptory.'' He also remarks that he was a great spendthrift in the matter of powder and gloves. So much his Lordship says of himself as to his foibles. One of his contemporaries has said of him, on his appearance in Parliament before the legal age: ''He is witty by nature, sometimes delightful, often severe; the wonder of his companions.'' His ambition was to excel in oratory and, according to Horace Walpole, it must have been gratified. He says, in a letter to Sir Horace Mann, that the finest speech he had ever heard was from Chesterfield. Sir Horace avers this after the statement that he had listened to all the orators of repute in his day. In many places in his writings Lord Chesterfield insists on the value of this accomplishment, for so he literally considered it and not essentially a gift of nature.

Diplomacy was especially attractive to him, and being twice Ambassador to Holland he thus had excellent opportunities for the exercise of his favorite *métier*. In this, Sir Watkins Winn—who was no friend—says of him, using Clarendon's dictum about another person, ''He has a head to contrive, a tongue to persuade, and a hand to execute any worthy action.'' So, it will be seen, Earl Chesterfield held a very high place in the estimation of *litterateurs* and politicians. But better things may be said to his credit. In an age when such things were rare, he had the humanity and courage to go against his colleagues in Parliament, and against public sentiment in urging a humane policy towards the Scotch Highlanders, lately in revolt for the Pretender, and to advocate the establishment of schools and other civilizing expedients among them. The tact, sagacity and humanity shown in his official career in Ireland were warmly commended at the time by Irishmen of distinction.

But the noble Earl's fate has been that of many who had the praise of their contemporaries. He has almost dropped out of the ken of the modern reader, so that of his writings it may be said, as he himself might have remarked of others in similar plight, *"l'oblië vaut le nouveau"*—for he was as facile in French as in English.

The portion of his writings that held place the longest were the letters to his son. Of these Doctor Samuel Johnson said that if certain objectionable features could be left out, he would wish to see them in the hands of every young man. It hardly needs being said that the Doctor's prescriptions have been followed in these selections.

This son was the issue of an alliance with a French-woman sometime previous to Lord Chesterfield's regular marriage in 1733 to Melusina de Schulemberg, the reputed niece of the Duchess of Kent.

The son reaped nothing from the painstaking sowing

of the father, but sank into excesses and obscurity. The letters were first published in 1774 by his widow. Various opinions have been expressed of Philip Dormer Stanhope and his writings, both by contemporaries and moderns. They are mostly damnatory, more especially of the man.

In reviewing his own career he said: "Call it vanity if you will, and possibly it was so, but my great object was to make every man I met like me, and every woman love me. I often succeeded, but why? By taking great pains." Probably the difficulty was that this was too apparent.

An admirable custom of his was never to let late hours or dissipation interfere with his serious studies. For forty years, he said, however late he went to bed, he was always up before nine o'clock in the morning, commonly before eight.

Lord Chesterfield was not so successful or brilliant in aphoristic composition as La Rochefoucauld, or so persistently cynical. The fact that the mordant sentences of the Frenchman are more familiar to English-speaking people than the aphorisms of the Englishman, is easily accounted for. The latter are only to be found on the perusal of the whole body of writings by the Earl, a task which the general reader would hardly undertake.

It was eminently characteristic of the man that the

last words he uttered should be ceremonious. "Give Dayrolles a chair," he said, faintly, when that friend called to inquire how his lordship did that morning.

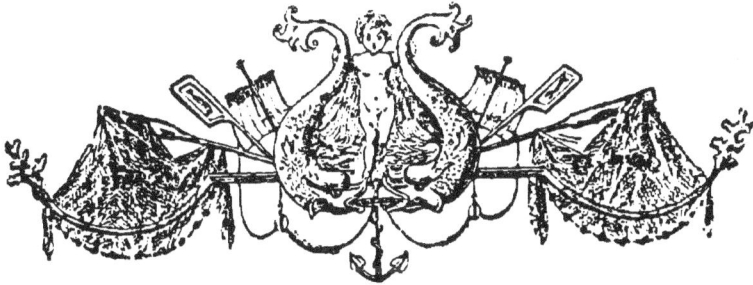

WORLDLY WISDOM

I.

NEXT to doing the things that deserve to be written, there is nothing that gets a man more credit, and gives him more pleasure, than to write the things that deserve to be read.

II.

GREAT Talents are above the generality of the world, who neither possess them themselves, nor judge of them rightly in others: but all People are Judges of the lesser talents, such as Civility, Affability, and an agreeable Address and Manner.

III.

I HARDLY know anything so difficult to attain, or so necessary to possess, as perfect good Breeding; which is equally inconsistent with a stiff Formality, an impertinent Forwardness, and an awkward Bashfulness. A little Ceremony is often necessary, a certain degree of Firmness is absolutely so.

IV.

DANCING in itself is a very trifling, silly thing; but it is one of those established Follies to which people of Sense are sometimes obliged to conform. . . . Dress is a very foolish thing, and yet it is a very foolish thing for a Man not to be well dressed, according to his rank and way of life; and it is so far from being a Disparagement to any Man's Understanding, that it is rather a Proof of it, to be as well dressed as those he lives with; the Difference in this case between a Man of sense and a Fop, is that a Fop values himself upon his Dress, and the man of Sense laughs at it: there are a thousand foolish Customs of this kind, which, not being criminal, must be complied with, and even cheerfully, by Men of Sense. Diogenes, the Cynic, was a wise Man for despising them, but a Fool for showing it. Be wiser than other People if you can, but do not tell them so.

V.

IF you can once engage People's Pride, Love, Pity, Ambition . . . on your Side, you need not fear what their Reason can do against you.

VI.

THE Desire of pleasing is at least half the Art of doing it.

VII.

WHEN you have found out the prevailing Passion of any Man, remember not to trust him where that Passion is concerned.

VIII.

LAZINESS, Inattention and Indifference are faults which are only pardonable in old men, who, in the Decline of Life, when Health and Spirits fail, have a Claim to that sort of Tranquillity.

IX.

HOWEVER frivolous a Company may be, still, when you are among them, do not show them by your Inattention, that you think them so.

X.

A MAN is fit for neither Business nor Pleasure, who either cannot or does not command and direct his Attention to the present Object, and banish for that time all other objects from his thoughts.

XI.

I DO not wonder that you were surprised at the Credulity and Superstition at Einsiedlin (a German town at which Miracles were claimed to be performed). But remember, at the same time, that Errors and Mistakes, however gross, in Matters of Opinion, if they are sincere, are to be pitied, but not punished, nor laughed at. The Blindness of the Understanding is as much to be pitied as the Blindness of the Eye,

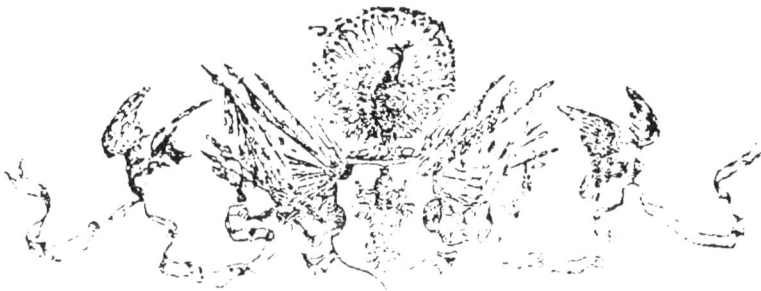

and there is neither Jest nor Guilt in a Man's losing his Way in either Case. Charity bids us to set him right if we can, by Argument and Persuasion; but Charity, at the same time, forbids either to punish or ridicule his Misfortune. Every Man's reason is, and must be, his Guide, and I may as well expect, that every Man should be of my size and Complexion, as that he should reason just as I do. Every man seeks for Truth, but God only knows who has found it. It is therefore as unjust to persecute as it is absurd to ridicule People for those several Opinions which they cannot help entertaining from convictions of their Reason.

XII.

I REALLY know nothing more criminal, more mean, more ridiculous, than Lying. It is the Production of either Malice, Cowardice or Vanity.

XIII.

CONCEALED Cowards will insult known ones.

XIV.

FOR my own Part, I judge of every Man's Truth by his degree of Understanding.

XV.

WHAT I mean by low Company, which should by all means be avoided, is the Company of those who, absolutely insignificant and contemptible in themselves, think they are honored by being in your Company; who flatter every Vice and every Folly you have in order to engage you to converse with them.

XVI.

THE Scholar without good Breeding, is a Pedant; the Philosopher a Cynic; the Soldier a Brute; and every man disagreeable.

XVII.

THE Pride of being first of the Company is but too common; but it is very silly, and very prejudicial. Nothing in the World lets down a Character more than that wrong turn.

XVIII.

DO not tell Stories in Company; there is nothing more tedious and more disagreeable.

XIX.

REMEMBER that there is a local Propriety to be observed in all Companies.

XX.

IF a Man has a mind to be thought wiser, and a Woman handsomer than they really are, their Error is a comfortable one to themselves, and an innocent one with regard to other People; and I would rather make them my Friends by indulging them in it,

19

than my Enemies by endeavoring (and that to no purpose) to undeceive them.

XXI.

I BELIEVE there is more Judgement required for proper Conduct of our Virtues, than for avoiding their opposite Vices.

XXII.

THOSE who travel heedlessly from place to place, observing only their distance from each other, and attending only to their accommodation at the Inn at night, set out Fools, and will certainly return so.

XXIII.

TRUE Friendship requires certain Proportions of Age and Manners, and can never subsist where they are extremely different, except in the relation of Parent and Child.

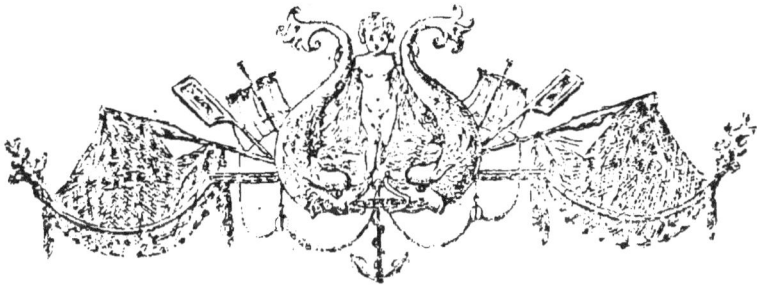

NEVER seem wiser, or more learned than the People you are with.

A COMMON Topic for false Wit, and cold Raillery is Matrimony. I presume that Men and their Wives neither love nor hate each other more, upon account of the Form of Matrimony that has been said over them.

THE characteristic of a well-bred Man is to converse with his inferiors without Insolence, and with his Superiors with respect and with Ease. He talks to Kings without Concern; he trifles with Women of the first Condition, with Familiarity and Gaiety, but Respect.

HIS Holiness is actually little more than the Bishop of Rome with large Temporalities,

which he is not likely to keep longer than 'till the other great Powers of Italy shall find their Conveniency in taking them from him. (Written 1748.)

XXVIII.

AWKWARDNESS of Carriage is very alienating, and a total Negligence of Dress and Air is an impertinent Insult upon Custom and Fashion.

XXIX.

WRONGS are often forgiven, but Contempt never is; our Pride remembers it forever: it implies a discovery of Weaknesses which we are more careful to conceal than Crimes.

XXX.

A SPRUCENESS of Dress is very becoming at your Age; as the Negligence of it implies an Indifferency about pleasing, which does not become a young Fellow.

XXXI.

THERE are two Sorts of Understandings, one of which hinders a man from ever being Considerable, and the other commonly makes him ridiculous, I mean the lazy Mind, and the trifling, frivolous Mind.

XXXII.

THINGS in the common Course of Life depend entirely upon the Manner; and in that respect the vulgar Saying is true, "That one man may better steal a Horse than another look over a Hedge." There are few things that may not be said in some Manner or other, either in seeming Confidence, or genteel Irony; or introduced with Wit; and one great Part of the knowledge of the World, consists in knowing when and where to make use of these different Manners.

XXXIII.

GIVE me but virtuous Actions, and I will not quibble and chicane about the Motives.

XXXIV.

AS Women are a considerable, or, at least, a pretty numerous Part of Company; and as their Suffrages go a long Way towards establishing a man's character in the fashionable Part of the World (which is of great Importance to the Fortune and Figure he proposes to make in it), it is necessary to please them.

XXXV.

YOU may safely flatter any Woman, from her Understanding down to the exquisite Taste of her Fan.

XXXVI.

WOMEN who are either exquisitely beautiful or indisputably ugly, are best flattered upon

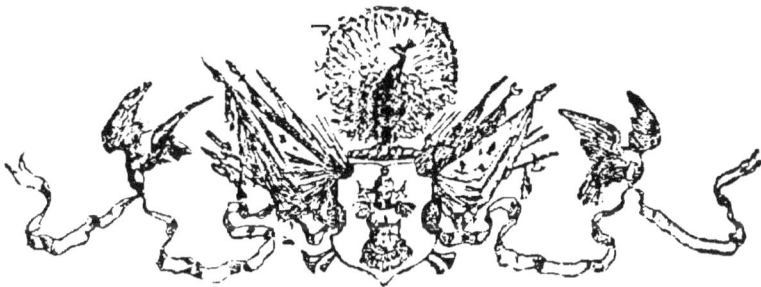

the score of their Understandings; but those who are in a State of Mediocrity, are best flattered upon their Beauty, or at least their Graces; for every Woman who is not absolutely ugly thinks herself handsome; but not hearing often that she is so, is the more gratified and the more obliged to the few who tell her so; Whereas a decided and conscious Beauty, looks to every Tribute paid to her Beauty as only her due; but wants to shine and be considered on the Side of her Understanding; and a Woman who is ugly enough to know that she is so, knows that she has nothing left for it but her Understanding, which is consequently (and probably in more senses than one) her weak side. . . . They have, from the Weakness of Men, more or less influence in all Courts; they absolutely stamp every Man's Character in the *Beau Monde*, and make it either current, or cry it down, and stop it in payments.

XXXVII.

EVERY man is not ambitious, or covetous or passionate, but every man has pride enough in his Composition to feel and resent the least Slight and Contempt. Remember therefore most carefully to conceal your, Contempt, however just, wherever you would not make an implacable Enemy

XXXVIII.

NEVER yield to that Temptation which to most young Men is very strong, of exposing other people's Weaknesses and Infirmities, for the Sake either of diverting the Company or of showing your own Superiority.

XXXIX.

OBSERVE any Meetings of People, and you will always find their Eagerness and Impetuosity rise or fall in Proportion to their Numbers: when Numbers are very great all sense of Reason seems to

subside, and one Sudden Phrenzy to seize all, even the coolest of them.

XL.

CARDINAL DE RETZ says: "that he is persuaded that, when Caligula made his Horse a Consul, the People of Rome at that Time were not greatly surprised at it, having necessarily been in some degree prepared for it, by an insensible gradation of Extravagances from the same quarter." This is so true that we read Every Day with Astonishment, things which we see Every Day without surprise. We wonder Every Day at the Intrepidity of a Leonidas, a Codrus and a Curtius, and are not the least surprised to hear of a Sea Captain who has blown up his Ship, his Crew and Himself, that they might not fall into the hands of the Enemies of his Country.

XLI.

I WOULD have you dance a Minuet very well— not so much for the sake of the Minuet itself

(though that if danced at all ought to be danced well), as that it will give you an habitual genteel carriage and manner of presenting yourself.

XLII.

PRAY let no quibble of Lawyers, nor Refinements of Casuists break into the plain Notions of Right and Wrong, which Every Man's right Reason and plain Common Sense suggest to him.

XLIII.

TO do as you would be done by is the plain, sure and undisputed Rule of Morality and Justice. Stick to that, and be convinced that whatever breaks into it in any Degree, however speciously it may be turned, and however puzzling it may be to answer it, is, notwithstanding, false in itself, unjust and criminal.

XLIV.

GOOD Company is not what respective Sets of Company are pleased either to call or think themselves, but it is that Company which all the

People of the Place call and acknowledge to be good Company, notwithstanding some objections which they may form to some of the People who compose it.

XLV.

THE Company of professed Wits and Poets is extremely inviting to most young men, who, if they have Wit themselves, are pleased with it, and if they have none are sillily proud of being of it; but it should be frequented with Moderation and Judgement, and you should by no means give yourself up to it.

XLVI.

BE your character what it will, it will be known and nobody will take it upon your own Word.

XLVII.

FLIMSEY parts, little Knowledge, and less Merit, introduced by the Graces have been received, cherished and admired. Even Virtue, which is moral Beauty, wants some of its Charms if unaccompanied by them.

29

XLVIII.

OF all the Men that I ever knew in my Life (and I knew him well), the late Duke of Marlborough possessed the Graces in the highest Degree, not to say Engrossed them; and indeed, got the most by them; for I will venture (contrary to the Custom of profound Historians, who always assign deep causes for great events) to ascribe the better Half of the Duke of Marlborough's Greatness and Riches to these Graces. He was eminently illiterate; wrote bad English and spelt it worse. He had no share of what is commonly called Parts; that is, he had no brightness, nothing shining in his Genius. He had undoubtedly an excellent, good, plain understanding with sound Judgement; . . . could refuse more gracefully than other People could grant, and those who went away from him the most dissatisfied, as to the substance of their Business, were yet personally charmed with him, and in some Degree comforted by his manners.

30

XLIX.

A MAN of Sense carefully avoids any particular Character in his Dress; he is accurately clean for his own Sake, but all the Rest is for other People's. He dresses as well, and in the same Manner as the People of Sense and Fashion of the Place where he is. If he dresses better, as he thinks, that is, more than they, he is a Fop; if he dresses worse, he is unpardonably negligent: but of the Two, I would rather have a Young Fellow too much, than too little dressed: the Excess on that side will wear off with a little Age and Reflection; but if he is negligent at Twenty, he will be slovenly at Forty, and stink at Fifty Years old.

L.

A FOOL squanders away without credit or advantage to himself, more than a Man of Sense spends with both.

LI.

UNDER the head of rational Pleasures, I compre-
hend, first, proper Charities to real and com-
passionate Objects of it; secondly, proper Presents to
those to whom you are obliged; or whom you desire
to oblige; thirdly, a Conformity of Expense to that of
the Company which you keep.

LII.

IN Economy, as well as in every other Part of Life
. . . have the proper Attention to proper Objects, and the proper Contempt for little ones.

LIII.

THE sure Characteristic of a sound and strong
Mind, is to find in Everything these certain
Bounds, *"quos ultra citrave nequit consistere rectum."*
The Boundaries are marked out by a very fine Line, which
only good sense and Attention can discover; it is much
too fine for vulgar Eyes. In manners, this Line is good

32

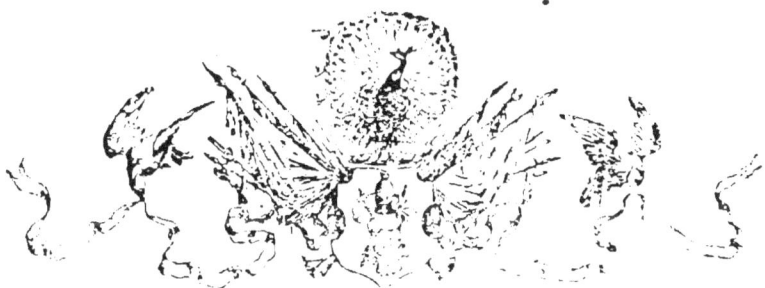

Breeding: beyond it is troublesome Ceremony; short of it is unbecoming Negligence and Inattention. In Morals it divides ostentatious Puritanism, from criminal Relaxation. In Religion, Superstition from Impiety.

LIV.

I ASSERT (speaking of Paradise Lost) with Mr. Dryden, that the Devil is in Truth the Hero of Milton's poem; his Plan which he lays, pursues and at last executes, is the Subject of the Poem.

LV.

THE Man who cannot join Business and Pleasure, is either a formal Coxcomb in one, or a sensual Beast in the other.

LVI.

IT has been long said *"qui nescit dissimulare nescit regnare."* I will go further and say that, without some Dissimulation no Business can be carried on at all. It is *Simulation* that is false and mean and crim-

33

inal; that is the Cunning which Lord Bacon calls crooked or left-handed Wisdom.

LVII.

SOME People are to be reasoned, some flattered and some intimidated and some teazed into a thing . . . The Time should likewise be judiciously chosen. Every man has his *Mollia Tempora*, but that is far from being all day long; and you would choose your Time very ill, if you applied to a man about one Business, when his head is full of another, or when his heart was full of Grief, Anger, or any other disagreeable Sentiment.

LVIII.

THE Temptation of saying a smart or witty Thing or *bon mot*, and the malicious Applause with which it is commonly received has made more People who can say them, and still oftener, People who think they can, but cannot, yet try, more Enemies than any other one Thing that I know of.

34

LIX.

THERE is a certain Dignity of Manners absolutely necessary, to make even the most valuable Characters either respected or respectable.

LX.

INDISCRIMINATE Familiarity either offends your superiors, or else dubs you their dependant and led Captain. It gives your Inferiors just, but troublesome and improper Claims of Equality.

LXI.

WHOEVER is admitted or sought for in Company, upon any other Account but that of his Merit and Manners, is never respected there, but only made use of.

LXII.

DIGNITY of Manners . . . is not only different from Pride—as true Courage is from Blustering, and true Wit from Joking—but is absolutely

35

inconsistent with it; for nothing vilifies and degrades more than Pride.

W HOEVER is in a hurry, shows that the Thing that he is about to do is too big for him. Haste and Hurry are very different Things.

I T is of no sort of Purpose to talk to those People (*i. e.*, the adherents of the Pretender on the Continent) of the natural Rights of Mankind, and the particular constitution of this Country. Blinded by Prejudice, soured by Misfortunes, and tempted by Necessities, they are incapable of reasoning rightly, as they are of acting wisely. The late Lord Pembroke would never know anything that he had not a mind to know; and in this Case I advise you to follow his Example. Never know either the Father, or the two sons (Charles Edward and Henry, Cardinal of York) otherwise than as foreigners, and so, not knowing·

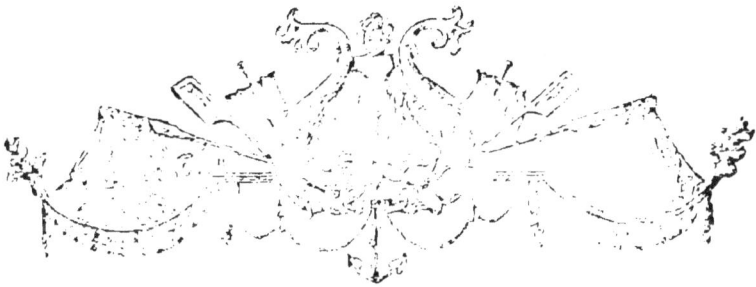

their Pretentions, you have no occasion to dispute them.

LXV.

APROPOS of the Pope. Remember to be presented to him before you leave Rome, and go through the necessary Ceremonies for it, Even to Kissing the Slipper . . . I would never deprive myself of anything I wished to do or see, by refusing to comply with an established Custom . . . (it is) a complaisance due . . . and by no Means, as Some People have imagined, an implied Approbation of their Doctrine. Bodily Attitudes and Situations are Things so very indifferent in themselves, that I would quarrel with Nobody about them.

LXVI.

WITH weak People (and they are undoubtedly three Parts in four of Mankind) good Breeding and Address are everything; they can go no deeper: but let me assure you, they are a great deal even with People of the best Understandings.

LXVII.

STYLE is the Dress of Thoughts . . . it is not Every Understanding that can Judge of Matter, but Every Ear can and does judge more or less of style.

LXVIII.

ENGAGE the Eyes by your Address, Air and Motions; soothe the Ears by the Elegance and Harmony of your Diction, the Heart will certainly follow, and the whole Man or Woman will as certainly follow the Heart.

LXIX.

I HAVE often thought, and still think that there are few Things which People know less than how to love and how to hate. They hurt those they love by a mistaken Indulgence, by a Blindness, nay a Partiality to their Faults. Where they hate, they hurt themselves by ill-timed Passion and Rage.

LXX.

I HAVE known many a Man undone by acquiring a ridiculous nick-name.

LXXI.

IF you will please People, you must please them in their own Way; and, as you cannot make them what they should be, you must take them as they are.

LXXII.

THE same Matter occurs equally to Everybody of Common Sense, upon the same question; the dressing it well is what excites the Attention and Admiration of the Audience.

LXXIII.

I HAVE spoken frequently in Parliament, and not always without some Applause, and therefore I can assure you from my Experience, that there is very little in it. The Elegancy of the style, the turn of the

periods make the chief impression upon the Hearers.
Give them but one or two sound and harmonious
Periods in a Speech, which they will retain and re-
peat, and they will go home as well satisfied as People from an Opera, humming all the way one or two
favourite Tunes which have struck their ears—and
were easily caught. Many People have Ears, but few
have Judgement; tickle those Ears, and depend upon
it, you will catch their Judgements, such as they are.

LXXIV.

WOMEN are much more like each other than
Men.

LXXV.

I WOULD not advise you to depend so much on
the heroic Virtue of Mankind, as to hope or
believe that your competitor will ever be your friend
as to the object of that Competition.

LXXVI.

GREAT Talents, and great Virtues, will procure
you the Respect and Admiration of Mankind;

but it is the lesser Talents, the *leniories virtutes* which must procure you their Love and Affection.

LXXVII.

YOU should by no means seem to approve, encourage or applaud those libertine Notions which strike at religions equally, which are poor threadbare Topics of Half-Wits and minute Philosophers. Even those who are silly enough to laugh at their Jokes, are still wise enough to distrust and detest their Characters; for, putting moral virtues at their highest, and Religion at the lowest, Religion must still be allowed to be a collateral Security, at least, to Virtue; and every prudent man will sooner trust to two securities than one.

LXXVIII.

DEPEND upon this Truth, that every man is the worse looked upon and the less trusted for being thought to have no Religion.

41

LXXIX.

YOUR moral Character must not only be pure, but like Caesar's wife, unsuspected. The least speck or blemish upon it is fatal. Nothing degrades and vilifies more, for it excites and unites Detestation and Contempt. There are, however, wretches in the world profligate enough to explode all Notions of Moral Good and Evil; to maintain that they are merely local and depend entirely upon the Customs and Fashions of different countries, nay, there are still, if possible, more unaccountable wretches; I mean those who affect to preach and propagate such infamous notions without believing them themselves. These are the Devil's Hypocrites. . . . As you may, by accident, fall into such Company, take great care that no Complaisance, no good Humour, no warmth of festal Mirth, ever make you seem to acquiesce, much less to approve or applaud such doctrines.

LXXX.

THERE is one of the Vices into which People of good Education and, in the main, of good Principle, sometimes fall from mistaken notions of Skill, Dexterity and Self-Defense; I mean Lying; though it is inseparably attended with more Infamy and Loss than any other. The Prudence and Necessity of often concealing the Truth seduces people to violate it. It is the only Art of mean Capacities and the only Refuge of mean Spirits.

LXXXI.

DEFAMATION and Calumny never attack where there is no weak place; they magnify, but they do not create.

LXXXII.

THERE is a sort of veteran woman of Condition who, having always lived in the *grand monde*
. . . with the Experience of five-and-twenty or thirty

years, forms a Young Fellow better than all the Rules that can be given him. . . . They will point out to you those Manners and Attentions that pleased and engaged them when they were in the Pride of their Youth and Beauty. Ask their Advice . . . but take care not to drop one word of their Experience; for Experience implies Age, and the Suspicion of Age no woman, let her be ever (*sic*) so old, ever forgives.

LXXXIII.

THE Pleasures that you would feel, you must earn; the man who gives himself up to all feels none sensibly.

LXXXIV.

THOSE only who Join serious Occupations with Pleasures feel either as they should do.

LXXXV.

THEY (*i. e.*, the devotees to the Pleasures of life only) are only so many human Sacrifices to false Gods.   44

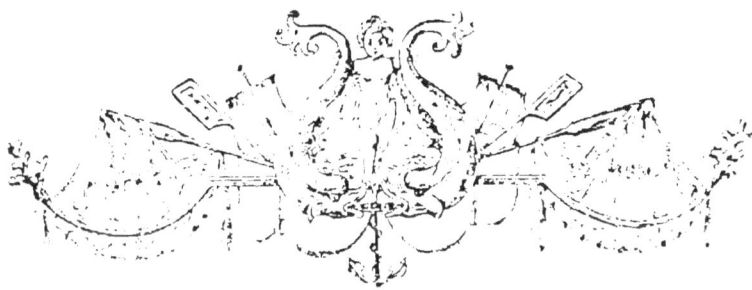

LXXXVI.

THE little Frailties of Youth flowing from high Spirits and warm Blood . . . certainly mend by Time, often by Reason; and a Man's worldly Character is not affected by them, provided it be pure in all other respects.

LXXXVII.

MODESTY is the only sure Bait when you angle for Praise.

LXXXVIII.

SENSE must distinguish between what is impossible and what is only difficult; Spirit and Perseverance will get the better of the latter.

LXXXIX.

IN all Courts you must expect to meet Connections without Friendships, Enmities without Hatred, Honour without Virtue, Appearances saved and Realities sacrificed, good Manners with bad Morals, and

all Vice and Virtue so disguised, that whoever has
only reasoned upon both, would know neither when
he first met them at Court.

XC.

I CAN assure you that it is no little help in the
Beau Monde to be puffed there by a fashionable
Woman.

XCI.

FROM the Moment that you are dressed and go
out, pocket all your Knowledge with your
Watch, and never pull it out in Company unless de-
sired: the producing of the one unasked implies that
you are weary of the Company, and the producing
of the other unrequired will make the Company weary
of you.

XCII.

WHATEVER is done under Concern and Em-
barrassment must be ill done; and 'till a man
is absolutely easy and unconcerned in every Com-

pany, he will never be thought to have kept good, nor to be very welcome in it.

XCIII.

A MAN of Sense takes the Time for doing the thing that he is about well: and his Haste to dispatch a Business only appears by the continuity of his application to it.

XCIV.

WE are so made we love to be pleased better than to be informed; Information is to a certain degree mortifying, as it implies our previous Ignorance: it must be sweetened to be palatable.

XCV.

I REMEMBER that when I came from Cambridge, I had acquired amongst the Pedants of that illiberal Seminary, a Sauciness of Literature, a Turn to Satire and Contempt, and a strong Tendency to Argumentation and Contradiction. But I had been

47

very little in the World when I found out that this would by no means do; and I immediately adopted the opposite Character: I concealed what Learning I had, I applauded often without approving; and I yielded commonly without Conviction.

XCVI.

FEW People have Penetration enough to discover, Attention enough to observe, or even Concern enough to examine, beyond the Exterior; they take their Motives from the surface and go no deeper.

XCVII.

HAPPY the Man who, with a certain Fund of Parts and Knowledge, gets acquainted with the World Early enough to make it his Bubble.

XCVIII.

USE Paliatives when you contradict.

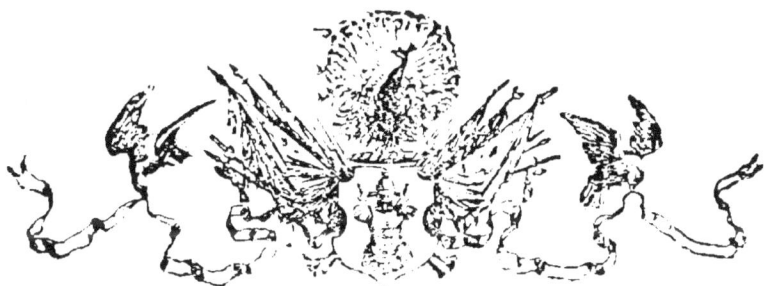

XCIX.

SOYEZ convaincu que la Femme la plus sage se trouve flattée, bein loni d'etre offensée par une Declaration d'Amour faite avec Politesse et Agrément.

C.

I ALWAYS treat Fools and Coxcombs with great-Ceremony; true good Breeding not being a sufficient Barrier against them.

CI.

KNOWLEDGE of the World teaches us more particularly two Things, both of which are of equal Consequence, and to neither of which Nature inclines us; I mean the command of our Temper, and of our countenance.

CII.

IT is a Shame and an Absurdity for any Man to say that he cannot do all of those things that are commonly done by the Rest of Mankind.

49

CIII.

PEOPLE seldom know how to employ their time to the best Advantage until they have too little left to employ.

CIV.

A YOUNG Fellow ought to be wiser than he should seem to be; and an old Fellow ought to seem wise whether he is so or not.

CV.

A FOREIGN Minister, I will maintain it, can never be a good Man of Business, if he is not an agreeable Man of Pleasure, too.

CVI.

ALL Acts of Civility are by Common Consent understood to be no more than a Conformity to custom for the quiet and conveniency of Society, the *agréments* of which are not to be disturbed by private dislikes and jealousies.

CVII.

I PROFESS myself an Ally of Turnus's against the pious Æneas, who, like many *soi-disant* pious People, does the most Flagrant Injustice and Violence in order to execute what they impudently call the Will of Heaven.

CVIII.

YOUNG Men are apt to think themselves wise enough, as drunken Men are apt to think themselves sober enough. They look upon spirit to be much better than Experience. I mean here by Spirit of Youth only the Vivacity and Presumption of Youth, which hinder them from seeing the Difficulties or Danger of an Undertaking.

CIX.

A WELL-BRED Man seldom thinks, and never seems to think, himself slighted or undervalued or laughed at in Company, unless where it is so plainly marked out that his Honour obliges him to resent it in a proper Manner.

CX.

A SEEMING Ignorance is very often a most necessary part of worldly Knowledge.

CXI.

FISH for Facts, and take Pains to be well informed of everything that passes; but fish judiciously.

CXII.

A PROPER Secrecy is the only Mystery of able Men; Mystery is the only Secrecy of Weak and Cunning Ones.

CXIII.

DISTRUST those who love you extremely and upon a very slight Acquaintance and with out visible Reason. Be on your guard, too, against those who confess as their Weaknesses all the Cardinal Virtues.

CXIV.

WHEN a Man of Sense finds himself in that Situation in which he is obliged to ask himself more than once, "What shall I do?" when his reason

points out to him no good way, or at least no one way less bad than another, he will stop short and wait for Light. A little busy mind runs on at all Events; must be doing, and, like a blind horse, fears no danger because he sees none. *Il faut sçavoir s'ennuyer.*

CXV.

A DIFFERENCE of Opinion, though in merest Trifles, alienates little Minds, especially of high Rank.

CXVI.

A MAN'S good Breeding is his best Security against other Peoples' ill Manners.

CXVII.

M OST Arts require long study and application; but the most useful of all, that of pleasing, requires only the desire.

CXVIII.

A SKILLFUL Negociator will most carefully distinguish between the little and the great objects

of his Business; and will be as frank and open in the former, as he will be secret and pertinacious in the latter.

CXIX.

THE preposterous Notions of a systematical Man who does not know the World, tire the Patience of a Man who does.

CXX.

I AM not only persuaded by Theory, but convinced by my experience, that (supposing a certain Degree of Common Sense) what is called a good Speaker is as much a Mechanic as a good Shoemaker; and that the two trades are equally to be learned by the same Degree of Application.

CXXI.

STATESMEN and Beauties are very rarely sensible of the gradations of their Decay, and, too sanguinely hoping to shine in their Meridian, often set with Contempt and Ridicule.

CXXII.

I LOOK upon Indolence as a sort of Suicide; for the Man is effectually destroyed, though the appetites of the Brute may survive.

CXXIII.

B USINESS by no Means forbids Pleasures; on the contrary they reciprocally season each other. I will venture to affirm that no Man enjoys either in Perfection that does not join in both.

CXXIV.

P ERSEVERANCE has surprising effects.

CXXV.

L ET us, then, not only scatter Benefits, but even strew flowers for our fellow Travellers, in the rugged Ways of this wretched World.

CXXVI.

A CERTAIN Degree of Ceremony is a necessary outwork of Manners as well as of Religion. It

keeps the forward and the petulant at a proper Distance, and is a very small Restraint to the sensible and well-bred part of the World.

CXXVII.

A WISE Man will live at least as much within his Wit as his Income.

CXXVIII.

VANITY is the more odious and shocking to Everybody, because Everybody, without exception, has Vanity; and two Vanities can never love one another any more than two of a Trade can.

CXXIX.

THERE are but two Objects in Marriage, Love and Money. If you marry for Love you will certainly have some very happy Days, and probably many very uneasy ones; if for Money, you will have no happy days, and probably no uneasy ones.

CXXX.

GIVE nobly to indigent Merit and do not refuse your Charity, even to those who have no Merit but their Misery.

CXXXI.

THE Manner makes the whole Difference. What would be Impudence in one Man is only a proper and decent Assurance in Another. A Man of Sense and Knowledge of the World will assert his own rights and pursue his own Objects, as steadily and intrepidly as the most Impudent Man Living, and commonly more so, but then he has art enough to give an outward Air of Modesty to all he does.

CXXXII.

WHEN they (young men) come to be a little better acquainted with themselves, and with their own Species, they discover that plain right Reason is nine times in ten, the fettered and shackled Attendant of the Triumph of the Heart and Passions;

consequently they addressed themselves nine times in ten, to the Conqueror and not to the Conquered.

CXXXIII.

A MAN who is really diffident, timid and bashful, be his Merit what it will, never can push himself in the world; his Despondency throws him into inaction; and the Forward, the Bustling and the Petulant will always get the better of him.

CXXXIV.

A MAN who tells nothing, or who tells all, will equally have nothing told him.

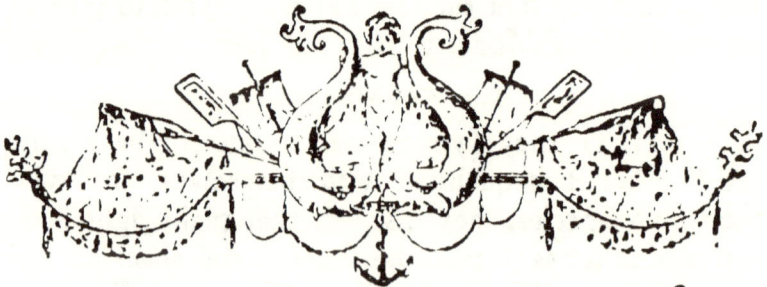